CUTTINGS

THE PICK OF
COUNTRY LIFE
FROM Punch

CUTTINGS

THE PICK OF
COUNTRY LIFE
FROM Punch

Compiled by Guy Pierce

Cartoons by Geoffrey Dickinson

ELM TREE BOOKS
LONDON

First published in Great Britain 1980
by Elm Tree Books/Hamish Hamilton Ltd
Garden House 57-59 Long Acre London WC2E 9JZ

Copyright © 1980 by Punch Publications Ltd
Cartoons copyright © 1980 by Geoff Dickinson

Book design by Glyn Rees

British Library Cataloguing in Publication Data

Cuttings.
   1.   English wit and humor
   I.   Pierce, Guy   II.   'Punch'
   827'.9'1408   PN6175
   ISBN 0-241-10496-3

Printed in Great Britain by
Richard Clay (The Chaucer Press) Ltd, Bungay, Suffolk

INTRODUCTION

Week in, week out, *Punch* is inundated with clippings from the provincial press – home and abroad – submitted by the magazine's readers for inclusion in the Country Life column. Not only is the abundance of mail welcome news for the Post Office's accountants but it also reflects the popularity of this *Punch* feature, which for the past twelve years has acted as a platform for the vagaries of local newspapers and periodicals – those 'scoops' which somehow slipped through the net of the 'nationals', be they typographical mishaps, inapt quotes, or pieces of news of such staggering inconsequence as to leave one wondering how they ever got further than a cub reporter's notebook.

Every Monday a *Punch* staffer ploughs his or her way through the mound of envelopes that is the Country Life 'in-tray', dutifully selecting the dozen or so gems that will make up the next issue's column.

There are no particular criteria to a successful Country Life contribution – if it's funny that's enough to warrant inclusion. If one thing has been learnt from the myriad clippings sent in by readers, though, it's that the ferret should replace the lion and bulldog as the nation's animal symbol. Here, then, by courtesy of Posts, Telegraphs, Clarions, Mirrors, Bugles, Tribunes, Mercurys, Heralds, Echos and Gleaners the whole world over, and illustrated by Geoff Dickinson, is 'Cuttings', the crème de la crème of *Punch*'s Country Life – dedicated to sub editors everywhere.

GUY PIERCE

More men than women are convicted of shoplifting. The majority of women shoplifters are aged between 25 and 35. "But," said Mr Shepherd "there was the case of the really old lady who collapsed in a supermarket and when an ambulance was called was found to be suffering from hyperthermia—caused by a frozen chicken under her hat."

V. Wood *(The Scotsman)*

At one time he was well up in the first 10 places but hitting a bride in Wales damaged the suspension and he dropped back.

N. Butlin *(Autosport)*

Ambulance men at Georgetown, Merthyr, who have to share two pairs of wellington boots between 19 of them, are hoping to end a 20-year fight for a pair each.

P. Herlihy *(South Wales Echo)*

A 36-year-old Irishman who hurled his shoe through a Perth shop window called police to retrieve it because he did not want to break the law and enter the building.

J. Thompson *(The Age)*

May Day greetings to all comrades in the Labour Movements. Divided we stand, united we fall. Littlehampton Labour Party.

A. Brunt *(Littlehampton Gazette)*

Backing-up Bernice and Sam is a strong cast and backstage crew all combining to make this an exciting opening sow.

Performances are on 16th, 17th and 18th October and booing starts on 15th September.

J. Thomson *(News Shopper)*

Joan of Arc probably suffered from brain damage which resulted in her visions, said Dr. Harold Palmer when he spoke to St. Albans and District Association of University Women.

D. H. Tallon *(Herts Advertiser)*

Councillor T. Witherspoon wondered what benefits came from conferences. He could not recall any benefit to the ratepayers from any conference he had been to.

M. Sleigh *(Wolverhampton Express & Star)*

Cemetery charges are to go up from June 1st but there will be a 50% reduction for pensioners.

P. Maloney *(West London Observer)*

He said it is unlikely pollution is the cause and the fish bore no outward signs of disease—"these fish are perfectly healthy, except that they're dead."

H. B. Smith *(Vancouver Sun)*

Wellington N.Z.—Motor accidents have replaced falling out of coconut trees as the most common cause of death in Pacific islands, according to a medical expert.

R. A. Eagleton *(South China Morning Post)*

A Bangor man who admitted using the same coin to obtain gas from the meter at his home for nearly a year told Bangor magistrates on Tuesday that he did it "on the spur of the moment."

P. Hollindale *(North Wales Chronicle)*

His friends noticed a marked "personality change" as jealousy became his overpowering emotion. He drank up to two bottles of whisky a day and even cheated at chess.

M. Sebba *(Hampstead Express)*

A man who never wants to see his work put into practice came to Luton last night.

T. Hopkins *(Luton Evening Post)*

The crime was discovered when Grieve arrived in a taxi at a scrap merchants in Milnbank Road, Dundee. Two plain-clothes police officers were on a routine visit to the premises. Grieve said to one of them: "Is it OK, there's no police about?" He then removed a sack from the boot.

R. G. Gray *(Dundee Evening Telegraph)*

Mr. L. Brittain of 3 Cedar Drive, Thornton-in-Cleveland asks us to say he has no connection with a manure smell in the village.

P. J. Ward
(Middlesbrough Evening Gazette)

"The baton had nails and chains in it," the fiscal added. "It was a contemporary yet medieval weapon. Dunn was found to have a steel comb which was twisted and distorted in his possession and Muir had a stone in each pocket of no geological interest."

R. G. Munton *(Largs & Millport News)*

The BBC filmed the destruction of Pulteney Road Bridge in Bath and rushed the film to the station for inclusion in the television news. The film couldn't go because the train couldn't go over the bridge they'd just filmed coming down.

P. H. B. Harris *(Bath & West Evening Chronicle)*

"My husband's mother was Hawaiian and we thought it might be nice to give the child a traditional name," said Mrs Seymour, the mum of a 2½-week-old Washington boy on why he was baptised Keaminuimakahahaikalani.

H. Jacobs *(Birmingham Evening Mail)*

A market stall has stopped selling bottles of invisible ink which it was claimed yesterday made holes in a boy's pyjamas and caused part of a carpet at his home to disappear.

M. E. Wigelworth *(Yorkshire Post)*

A man with a passion for gliding and skin diving is expected to be named as the next Mayor of Kidderminster.

D. M. Copp *(Birmingham Evening Mail)*

A woman who stole two pen and pencil sets told Hendon magistrates last week that one was a present for her probation officer.

V. B. Greene *(Finchley Press)*

The Prince of Wales spent last winter being renovated at a cost of more than £30,000 at British Rail's Swindon depot, and returned to Aberystwyth a week ago.

P. Soloman *(Western Mail)*

If the unemployed were made to work on road building schemes it would improve the country's road system and hasten the return of law and order. "That is what Hitler had to do," Councillor Sid Childs told Highley Parish Council last night, "at least he brought Germany back to common-sense." Mr Childs said he was thinking of the country as a whole and not just the Highley area, though the road between Bridgnorth and Highley would be a good place to start.

P. Gruar *(Shropshire Star)*

A recent radar speed trap at Silver End was obviously aimed at the working class, claimed Mr. Bill Webdale at last night's meeting of Witham Trades Council. "It was there at 8 a.m. There are not many Rolls-Royces or Jags about at that time," he said.

P. R. Dean *(Colchester Evening Gazette)*

"The girls in the show stripped to their G-strings but not me. I just helped them to get changed. It seemed a giggle at first, but it got a bit boring. If that's show business, it's more boring than exciting. I would rather be a vet."

A. Donnelly *(Nottingham Post)*

A man who danced naked through a wood was told by a Sheriff yesterday that the great god Pan never wore socks.

J. Williamson (*Glasgow Herald*)

The boy had listed among his 52 findings of guilt: burglary, theft, malicious wounding, killing animals in a pet shop and setting fire to a railway station. All the offences were committed before the boy was 15. But a social worker told magistrates about him: "These kids would not have such a bad record if the police would not keep arresting them."

D. M. Minors *(Sheffield Star)*

The Chairman, Ald. George Wardle, suggested that the sheep might stop if notices were erected saying: "Sheep must not eat gravel." But members felt that even if they were warned of the direst consequences, this would have little effect.

M. Wright *(Newcastle Journal)*

A young Formosan wrote 700 letters to his girlfriend. She is to marry the postman.

L. Scott *(Stoke Evening Sentinel)*

Mr. Gillard, who is 55, tackled the man but was knocked to the ground. His assailant ran off in the direction of Mesopotamia.

H. W. S. Pigott (*Oxford Times*)

Muhammad Ali was missing when his name was called in court at Kidderminster. Police had been unable to serve summonses on him alleging speeding and having no Excise licence, said Inspector Tim Davidson. "And I think the name could very well be fictitious," he told magistrates.

D. Owen *(Worcester Evening News)*

Insp. Muxlow said Steven told police he had had an argument with his girlfriend and wanted to "end it all". But the prosecution did not accept his story, said the inspector. Had Stevens intended committing suicide, he would not have chosen to jump in front of a stationary car.

P. Young *(Lincolnshire Echo)*

A boy took home a stolen cycle and was thrashed by his father and sent to bed. But next day when he wanted to put matters right by returning the cycle, he found his father had gone to work on it.

G. R. D. Buxton *(Derby Telegraph)*

A long-term study of contraceptive methods is highly favourable to the diaphragm, with researchers finding "no material risks" other than pregnancy.

D. Parish *(International Herald Tribune)*

Gents black overcoat, long length, worn by undertaker, now retired, good quality, but one shoulder slightly worn. Phone...

B. Draper *(Liverpool Post)*

When a disaster occurs, the Red Cross Society is always glad to help—especially money. But some gifts can cause embarrassment. When 200 cases of bras were sent as a well-meaning gift to Pakistan, the problem which they caused was solved by cutting them in half to make two rice bowls.

R. R. Williamson
(Palmers Green & Southgate Gazette)

You can still sit on Torbay beaches for free as long as your bottom touches the sand. Raise yourself up and you pay a shilling—whether you use the corporation's chair or your own. "I'm not surprised at the charge. Everything costs you under Labour," said Mrs Hermione Clapp, of Maidenway Road, Paignton. Told that the council is Conservative controlled, she reckoned: "They get orders from above."

E. Shave *(Paignton News)*

Crash courses available for those wishing to learn to drive very quickly.

R. V. Elliston *(Eastbourne Gazette)*

A man was banned by court order from going within 100 yards of his estranged wife's home—except on Fridays. The husband is a refuse collector and his Friday round takes him to empty the bins in Howard Road where his wife lives.

V. Holloway *(Birmingham Evening Mail)*

Cross-examined by Mr Quinn, witness said that someone called her husband "an Irish pig." She said he was not Irish.

P. L. Moreton (*Biddulph Chronicle*)

Police at Kidderminster, Worcestershire, are looking for thieves who broke into a factory and stole 17 miles of sausage skin.

C. Goundry *(The Scotsman)*

On reaching the age of 90, members of St Mary's Charlton Kings Mothers' Union branch will no longer pay subscriptions, but become life members.

D. Thomas *(Gloucestershire Echo)*

The famous vicar's father was Rev. Jacob Hawker, one time curate and vicar of Stratton, so Robert spent his younger years in the town. Many tales are told of his fiendish practical jokes. He once ran through the streets and entangled every house and door with twine. Mr Harry Yeo, chairman of the committee, proposed a vote of thanks.

H. E. Moore *(Bude & Stratton Post)*

The night after a young wife returned home without her skirt her husband made her eat a moth.

G. Hill (*Sheffield Star*)

Hong Kong's prosperity and gross national product are in the highest Asian bracket. So, it would seem natural that the socio-economic compulsions that force children into factories here are less strong here than in the poorer countries of the region. Evidently, somewhere in the Hong Kong way of life there is a chink.

A. Lockwood *(Straits Times)*

Police last night questioned 14 deaf and dumb youths about a robbery of a number of passengers on board a Kowloon bus.

G. Ireland
(Hong Kong South China Morning Post)

Mr Cyril Chitty, of Chichester, has retired after thirty years as one of the most successful rat catchers in West Sussex. An expert on moles and mice extermination, Mr Chitty bagged 200 rats in one day on a farm at Compton. He was a Desert Rat during the last war.

P. Hamilton *(Bognor Regis Post)*

Shepherd was sent to prison for a total of 12 months and was disqualified from driving for 12 months.

D. Stein *(Kingsbury News)*

When the Queen's great aunt, Princess Alice, met veteran Millwall fan Arthur Hodge, 74, who proudly wore the badge and bars of the supporters' club, she said she had never heard of the team.

R. Holmes *(South London Press)*

Mr. Kanso Yoshida, cousin of Emperor Hirohito of Japan, has died in Liverpool, aged 78. Since he came to Liverpool in 1912, Mr. Yoshida had been known as Paddy Murphy.

R. W. Branch *(Liverpool Post)*

Democrat MP Paitoon Wongvanich rides to Parliament yesterday on a buffalo. He only got as far as the main gate where a guard refused to allow the animal to enter. When Paitoon argued that cars were permitted inside the guard stolidly replied: "Yes, but they don't (excretive deleted)." J. C. J. Owens *(Bangkok Post)*

The parish council at Moreton-in-Marsh has decided that there is nothing it can do about a complaint that ducks from the town's duck pond are walking around with dirty feet.

J. Benton (*Birmingham Mail*)

The managing director of a textile mill at Mirfield, near Huddersfield, plans to breed llamas near the premises to combat a serious supply shortage.

J. M. Cochrane *(Yorkshire Post)*

Having read of a Wakering woman who died of hypothermia after a fall at her home I am prompted to write to you of my similar experience.

R. Allon-Smith *(Southend Standard)*

Mr. Spalding believed that the secret of his eternal youth lay in the fact that he had an early morning skipping session followed by a long walk, every day. The funeral takes place next Tuesday.

J. Earl (*Kentish Times*)

A prostitute with pink plastic curlers atop her head and carpet slippers on her feet did the merengue through the door and all the way to a can of Crisco. She picked it up, danced back to Mr. Polanco, and asked for a pack of Newport cigarettes. Then she paid, stuck out her tongue, put her thumbs in her ears, and wiggled her **Continued on page 47, Column 4.**
B. Ouellette (*New York Times*)

Florida.—The report said the primary problem of the "poor" and "near poor" is lack of adequate funds to meet their needs.
J. T. Leviston *(Today—Florida's Space Age Newspaper)*

Gordon Banks will be back in foal for Stoke by May—and it could be even sooner.   I. Roberts *(Western Mail)*

When Jimmy Carter, President of the United States and the world's most powerful man, comes to Britain next month he won't be visiting the small Oxfordshire village of Sulgrave.   N. Cottis *(Oxford Star)*

A group of Welsh Nationalists paraded outside the BBC's Birmingham headquarters during the lunchtime television broadcast of Pebble Mill yesterday. But officials did not know what they were protesting about as the placards were in Welsh.

T. Mann *(Birmingham Post)*

Ex. Southport F.C. chief Billy Bingham was to be seen putting his new team Everton through their paces on Ainsdale Beach earlier in the week. A meeting of toads has been called to discuss the problem.

Mrs. Sinnott
(*Southport and District Advertiser*)

Security at a Surrey hospital has been stepped up after a half-naked man broke in and assaulted a nurse. Windows have been reinforced and police are keeping a close watch on the geriatric wing of Dorking hospital since the incident.

S. Meredith (*Surrey Advertiser*)

What sort of rents do houses fetch? Within fairly clearly-defined limits, it varies from area to area.

A. J. Hodge *(Irish Times)*

Attendance at Forest Row Memorial Committee's annual meeting was up 100 per cent on last year—but still only five people were present.

D. Gadberry *(East Grinstead Observer)*

The two girls had earlier testified that they had been approached in Ayr Road, Prestwick, by a man who invited them to "jump on him, kick him and walk on him." They said that they had been offered £1 each by the man. They both identified him in court as Anderson, although one of them picked out the official court shorthand writer before being asked by the Procurator-Fiscal to have a more thorough look round.

D. E. Girdwood *(The Scotsman)*

Coun. H. Brentnall pointed out that a long time ago he suggested that Asians should be invited to this area. If this had been done they would have helped the building situation. "There are some very good builders among them," he added. "They built the Taj Mahal when all is said and done."

A. Job *(Teesdale Mercury)*

Protests by donkey owners and Muslims have caused a plan to introduce camel rides on the beach at Scarborough to be abandoned. The donkey owners feared it would harm their trade. The Muslims were upset because one of the six camels involved was called Muhammad.

J. G. Williamson *(Glasgow Herald)*

In a recent report of a competition held at one of Pontin's holiday camps it was inadvertently stated that it was for "elephant" grandmothers instead of elegant grandmothers. We apologise to Mrs Hilda Price who gained the third place for any embarrassment this may have caused.

G. O. Johnson *(Stockport Advertiser)*

A crime prevention campaign featuring "Batman" and "Robin" in Slough's Queensmere shopping centre ran into problems on Saturday. First the "Batmobile" and then the "Boy Wonder" costume were stolen.

T. Williams *(Windsor Express)*

Caroline Ann Janman (18), a Chichester girl, agreed that she had been mixing with bad company when she appeared before Chichester magistrates last week. J. Norman *(West Sussex Gazette)*

A man who pleaded guilty at Bradford City Court to being drunk was asked by the chairman what he had to say, and he replied, "I have just come out of hospital where I have been having treatment for my drinking, and I had a drink to see if they'd cured me."

R. Mosey *(Telegraph & Argus)*

A fifteen-year-old Croydon boy has been suspended by his head since last September because of his long hair.

A. Campbell *(Times Educational Supplement)*

12.00. Violence with Rev. Paul Oestreicher and Father William Burridge.

M. Elderson *(Kent Messenger)*

A man who pleaded guilty at Bradford City Court to being drunk was asked by the chairman what he had to say, and he replied, "I have just come out of hospital where I have been having treatment for my drinking, and I had a drink to see if they'd cured me."

R. Mosey *(Telegraph & Argus)*

A crucial meeting of the Shipley and Baildon Chamber of Trade to decide whether it should disband through lack of support was attended by only three members.

M. C. O'Regan *(Yorkshire Post)*

MBC OFFER OF THE WEEK. A free set of Bass guitar strings with every secondhand trumpet.

R. Swailes *(Melody Maker)*

Among the suggestions for the naming of a Stoke Poges Road was Elvis Presley Boulevard.

M. Payne *(Bucks Free Press)*

In the event of a nuclear attack, children will be given a day off school, says the Scottish Home and Health Department.

L. Phillips *(Scottish Express)*

Councillor Albert Boozer appeared at Chatham Court on Wednesday accused of driving with excess alcohol.

G. A. Graber *(Chatham, Rochester & Gillingham News)*

The Amadeus String Quartet was out of commission earlier this year after its leader, Norbert Brainin, accidentally sat on his thumb. ..

A. P. Fyffe *(The Scotsman)*

A Harrogate company was fined £100 with £26 costs yesterday for selling "chunky chicken breasts" with only one chunk.

P. G. Haywood *(Yorkshire Post)*

Contraceptive devices will not be fitted to pigeons in Bath, the Family Services committee decided last night. Mr Ronald Redston, chief public health inspector, said the birth control method was too expensive. The committee decided to stick to more conventional ways of keeping down the pigeon population.

P. Thompson (*Western Daily Press*)

When magistrates arrived at Bradford's No. 1 court, they were faced with an embarrassing problem. The door leading from the cells into the dock was jammed and no one could open it. The police tried and an engineer tried, and still the lock would not turn. Eventually, Tom Wall, 45, a defendant on a drunk and disorderly charge, came to the rescue. He kicked the door open and the court started its proceedings ten minutes late.

M. J. Robinson *(Yorkshire Post)*

Another notable local prize-winner was Mr J. H. Pearson, who displayed the best unclassified entry. All those who saw his entry agreed whole-heartedly that it could not be put in any classification. B. Hill *(Surrey Mirror)*

Managing director Sir Edward Fennessy handed over the cup. She had scored 50 points out of a possible 60 on a test which covered treatment of a pub customer who has injured his nose on a swing door and as a result of incorrect treatment from the barmaid has developed a coronary obstruction.

A. E. Wilkins *(Southend Standard)*

Mr Alec Spurway questioned whether British Rail's estimate that it would cost £100,000 to re-open the station was accurate and asked how the county planning officer, Mr John Barrow, came to the conclusion that 200 people a day might use the station. Mr Barrow said it was a guess.

J. H. Scott *(Wallingford Herald)*

In the rainier parts of the country it also rains for longer periods than in the drier parts.

G. B. Moreton
(*Building Research Station Digest*)

Another discussion took place at the Church House meeting when the humorous magazine *Punch* was condemned for being "rather Socialist". It was proposed to substitute the magazine in the reading room for the *Illustrated London News* or the *Methodist Recorder*. A decision will be finalised at the next meeting.

D. Pettiward *(Salisbury Journal)*

A Stafford clergyman's housekeeper, who says her ancestors used to eat priests, has received a merit award from the Pope.

C. Rautenberg *(Staffordshire Evening Sentinel)*

A motorist driving down Evesham Road in Crabbs Cross in the early hours of Sunday morning was surprised to see a man standing by the roadside naked except for a sheet "which he opened from time to time." A subsequent police search revealed nothing.

M. Price (*Redditch Indicator*)

An 18-year-old Glasgow youth arrested at Hampden Park on Saturday and charged with "bawling, shouting and screaming" was released yesterday pending further enquiries as he was said to be a deaf mute.

D. Hughes *(The Scotsman)*

A woman who was thrown over a banister by her son-in-law twice within minutes said last night: "We never were very close."

M. P. Morrison
(Scottish Express)

Inspector Tim Davidson, prosecuting, said Smith was one of a crowd of youths who refused to leave the Briars pub when asked to. He became abusive, used foul language and had to be forcibly arrested. Smith said that he wanted to be arrested so that he could get away from Kidderminster.

K. Hardiman *(Kidderminster Shuttle)*

Dartmouth's best known budgie is dead. Kami-Kazi Joey, who lost his legs when he dropped into a boiling pan of brussels sprouts, passed away on Saturday night. He was nearly 11 years old. Joey's life was not without turmoil. After losing his legs he became an alcoholic, being fond of brandy and port. Vets gave up all hope. Joey leaves two very upset owners, Irene and Paul Darby of Victoria Road.

A. D. Mitchener *(Dartmouth Chronicle)*

Gone are the days of senior boys flogging their juniors, while capital punishment by staff is undertaken to a much lesser degree than previously.

D. Arthur *(Stafford Newsletter)*

Rufus Owen Watts Sr. has been re-elected to the Halifax County Democratic Committee, but he won't serve his term. Watts has been dead for more than a year. County party Chairman Howard P. Anderson said Watts was re-elected because the committee has a policy of "not dumping" members who have served faithfully.

D. Goldberg *(Los Angeles Times)*

The mayor of Coburg, Cr Murray Gavin, said a planned champagne and sausage Australia Day Party, organised by the mayor of Brighton was "exhibitionist". "Such an event desecrates the meaning of Australia and degrades local government, however popular it may be with participants seeking to emulate Louis 16," Cr Gavin said.

J. Ryan *(Melbourne Herald)*

A man who set himself on fire in a fast-food restaurant was in critical condition in hospital yesterday. Witnesses said the man had doused himself with solvent outside and entered the restaurant because the wind kept blowing his lighter out.

M. Doughty *(Toronto Globe and Mail)*

Christianity is not dead in Sydney. Not when a bemused citizen can report that while shopping in a city jeweller's for a gold crucifix and chain for his sister's birthday the young assistant asked: "Yes, what sort would you like . . . one with a little man on it?"

E. Braithwaite *(Sydney Daily Telegraph)*

Also Cleavon Little, Gene Wilder in BLAZING SADDLES (AA). Week and Sat. at 8.25. Sunday at 8.25. No person admitted to any part of the programme.

M. Mann *(Epsom Herald)*

A minister exorcised a house in Sherborne, Dorset, after two women summoned Elvis Presley's spirit with a Ouija board. The women, suffering from shock, reported the appearance as Presley's first visit to Britain.

C. Collins *(Southend Evening Echo)*

When Bob Dylan sang: "The times, they are a changing" he may well have been thinking of the area covered by the Middlesex Chronicle. From Staines to Chiswick, Hampton to Heston the changes this century have been phenomenal.

I. Heath *(Middlesex Chronicle)*

OUTLOOK. Dry and warm, but cooler with some rain.

M. Brown *(Western Daily Press)*

"The Impoverished Manager and his Rewards" a one day conference at the Hilton Hotel. Fee £80 + VAT (including documentation, lunch, wine and light refreshments).

G. R. Dawson *(Charterhouse Japhet Financial Services Ltd.)*

Mr Philip Curl, defending both, said Golding lacked self-control and had a self-destructive streak in him. King was less gifted, he added.

G. Fagg *(Eastern Daily Press)*

SITUATION WANTED. Keen but out of work actor looking for non-appearing, non-speaking parts.

G. Fellows *(West Highland Free Press)*

The home-loving girl won an £800 holiday for two in Thailand with a 25p lottery ticket. Heather, a factory worker, said: "I'd rather take the money. Thailand doesn't appeal to me and I've already arranged to go to Cleethorpes."

J. Hemmings *(Sheffield Morning Telegraph)*

The crowd of 2000 were entertained at lunchtime by a variety of "uniquely Australian" competitions. They watched Mr C. Saisell of Sydney drink 20 ounces of beer in 3.35 seconds, setting a new record to win the Australian Open 20-Ounce Beer Drinking Championships. And Arnie Constable played "Please Release Me" on the gum-leaf to win the gum-leaf blowing section. Mrs Marlene Crawford won the husband-calling with a bellow of "Your dinner's ready. Come and get it—or else." Russell Farrant won the beer-bottle top throwing contest, breaking the old record by five metres.

R. Sawkins *(Brisbane Courier-Mail)*

RENT-FREE WEEK FOR TEN ANTS IN ENNERDALE.

A. Pennington *(The Whitehaven News)*

Staging their first Derby Panto are director Michael Napier-Brown and Musical Director Andy Jubb, though they have appeared in these capacities here on other productions. A familiar figure in the pit from previous pantos will be Mike Sillitoe on drugs and percussion.

P. Jeffery *(West Notts Weekly Review)*

Pope John Paul was created by cheering crows when he arrived by helicopter at the ancient monastery of Jasna Gora.

J. Harvey *(Nottingham Evening News)*

CHANGE OF NAME OF COMPANY. Notice is hereby given that "Autopsy Parts Limited" has changed its name to "Bread Supplies Limited".

R. Tilley *(New Zealand Gazette)*

A Padiham man who dived head first on to the sands at Blackpool was told by magistrates at the resort to go back home and try to straighten himself out.

C. Waine *(Lancashire Evening Telegraph)*

Ferrets were seen in a field near the entrance to Drax Power station a year or more ago, but it is understood that they were recovered by their owner. It is not known what attraction, if any, power plants have for ferrets, but there used to be some in the vicinity of Eggborough Power Station.

E. Wharton *(Selby Gazette and Herald)*

ESSEX—First innings
Denness c Roebuck b Breakwell.......... 39
East not out 63
McEwan not wanted 29
　　　　　　　Extras.............. 8

C. Brooks *(Leicester Mercury)*

Lucas produce a completely pointless distributor to fit most cars.

M. Atkins *(Hot Car)*

Syston police would like to hear from anyone who say anything suspicious.

C. Merrill *(Leicester Mercury)*

The mutilated "dog" found hanging from a tree in Bog Wood, near Penicuik, at the weekend was actually a fox, Lothian and Borders police reported yesterday. They are no longer anxious to hear from anyone who has lost a light-coloured whippet.

N. Braidwood *(The Scotsman)*

"If it's a draw at the end of the contest it'll be decided by whichever team wins most sections," said compere, ready wet and king of the ad-libbers, Terry Wogan.

P. Nettleton *(Edinburgh Evening News)*

Volunteers urgently needed to help stroke patients with speech problems.

E. Abbott *(Chorlton and Wilbrampton News)*

A woman arrested as a prostitute claimed that she was too short sighted to ply for trade. Mrs. Margaret Friend, 48, said she was blind in one eye and vision in the other was blurred. She told Southend magistrates: "I can only see if someone is right on top of me."

D. A. Pawson *(Southend Evening Echo)*

Darlington: Soccer club manager Billy Elliot and director John Hunt have presented season tickets to patients and staff from the town's Memorial Hospital psychiatric ward.

J. Conlon *(Northern Echo)*

The French prime minister Raymond Barre yesterday morning laid a wretch on the monument of the unknown soldier.

D. Johnson *(Baghdad Observer)*

The family of an illiterate man cut off his thumb after he died, preserved it in formaldehyde and used the thumb for years to cash his pension cheques, an association of private investigators says.

J. Shaw *(Victoria Times)*

One dozen Mothercare shaped nappies (purchased by mistake), used once, £6.   J. Butterworth *(Oxford Mail)*

He was married for a short while to Marilyn Monroe, a genuine screen siren, but they were divorced when she committed suicide in 1962.

D. Marshall *(Vancouver Province)*

Football violence has been a growing menace in the United Kingdom but police are determined to get tough about it. They spoil it for everybody else.

W. Watts *(Cyprus Mail)*

French Catholics seem divided as to whether the Church is a united or divided Church. Fifty per cent said they thought the church was united, 42 per cent that it was divided.

A. Nevard *(Catholic Herald)*

Usually the information given in your magazine is concise and accurate, but your article on Circumcision (November 1978) left certain points uncovered.

J. Colman *(Letters Column, Mother Magazine)*

A Kidderminster man caught trying to take away a car had a suspicious bulge under his shirt, Inspector Aubrey Wallis told Kidderminster magistrates.

N. Patel *(Wolverhampton Express and Star)*

Hans Mulliken, a 39-year-old lay baptist minister who crawled 1600 miles on his knees from Texas to Washington, was told when he arrived at the gates of the White House the President was too busy to see him.

T. McCormick *(Glasgow Herald)*

"I didn't realize he was the Shah at first—he wasn't introduced as such—but we hit it off immediately. And later in the evening he suggested that I stay in Tehran and we see nothing of each other. So I did." A. Clark *(Victoria Times)*

Wards could be closed down during the summer, abortions limited to people living in and around the county and dying people discouraged from long stays in hospital.

A. Farrant *(Oxford Mail)*

The Leicester group of the National Schizophrenic Fellowship recently held two well-attended events at St James the Greater Church Hall, London Road, Leicester.

M. Hewitt *(Leicester Mercury)*

A pig herdsman is required at Crouchfield, a community home for 88 boys aged 15 to 17 years.

M. Clarke *(Farmers' Weekly)*

Why not have the kids shot for Easter, or have a family portrait taken. What have you to lose?

M. Bell *(Herts Mid Week Times)*

An Indonesian MP has offered advice to 2,000 prostitutes from a Jakarta red light district. "Never marry one of your customers," he told the women. "It is clear that the morality of these men is in doubt."

C. Hampton *(Bangkok Post)*

A man indecently exposed himself to a 12-year-old girl in Grattons Park, Pound Hill, on Tuesday evening last week. Police said he was about 40 with a black beard and short curly black hair, and short curly black hair.

M. McClelland *(Crawley Observer)*

The Yorkshire Ripper, West Yorkshire's Mr George Oldfield, has been ordered to take a "complete rest."

R. Malby *(Western Morning News)*

SEX ON DOORSTEP UPSETS OLD FOLK.

N. Bush *(Worksop Guardian)*

Bird told police: "I gave her a good hiding alright. I should have given her a better one. I did it because she had dyed blonde hair and I could see the roots. We are all barbarians up in Scotland. We're always getting into taxis and kicking people. Of course I hit her for nothing, but she deserved it. She gave me no reason whatsoever."

A. Gowing (*Hartlepool Mail*)

ITN newscaster Reginald Bosanquet upset cat lovers last night when he ended News at Ten with a story about the Army rescuing an old woman's cat from a tree in London. After being given tea and biscuits by the woman, the soldiers accidentally run over the cat in their Green Goddess.

E. Alcock (*Cleveland Evening Gazette*)

We apologise profusely to all our patrons who received, through unfortunate computer error, the chest measurements of members of Female Wrestlers Association instead of the figures on sales of soybeans to foreign countries.

L. Brent (*Saturday Review*)

British Rail are looking at the idea of improving the service between Luton and London by making more trains stop at Luton.

T. Hopkins (*Luton Evening Post*)

PLUMBING. New installations, repairs to old, approved by Age Concern.

B. Langman (*Leicester Mercury*)

"It is my very strong view that it would be most inappropriate for any non-maligned nation to attend the Moscow Olympics while Soviet troops are in Afghanistan."

A. Hopkins (*Lancashire Evening Post*)

International Schizophrenic Group Research requires part-time audio/secretary.

S. Dawson (*Time Out*)

A youth seen urinating in a beer glass at a Hemel Hempstead pub and steakhouse later told police he did not think much of the beer anyway, the town's magistrates were told.

C. Heathcote (*Hemel Hempstead Gazette*)

On leaving Cambridge Allister Goulding, an English graduate, spent three years working on construction sites. He is now writing a book on Chinese gang warfare.　　　　J. Gerrard (*The Architect*)

Farmer Obeid Abu Ali died at the age of 136 when he fell off the roof of his village home near Baghdad. Twice married, he left 170 children, the eldest aged 86. They were not all legitimate.

H. Stone *(Yorkshire Post)*

The British and American proposals for a transfer to majority rule provides for a United Nations force to supervise a cease fire during a six months transitional period to independence and, a constitution based on universal suffering.

G. Moore *(New Nigerian)*

Wengryn, a Pole who speaks very little English, had an interpreter in court. Recorder Mr Michael Kempster QC asked him if he had anything to say, but he did not.

T. Hopkins *(Luton Evening Post)*

And when the results were announced the lads were delighted. Paul won a gold for his tureen of game; Lawrence took a silver with his cold lobster and crayfish; Robert's trout brought him a silver; and Christ won a High Recommendation in the whitefish section with his turbot.

A. Bellis *(Bournemouth Bugle)*

David Thomas, lead singer of the rock group Blood, Sweat and Tears, has been arrested and charged with the sexual battery of a Florida woman.

C. Bohn *(Evening Standard)*

A letter from Mrs Saphouse, Felixstowe, asks if anyone remembers the statue of Queen Victoria and loins that once guarded the entry of Christchurch Park.

R. Meehan *(Ipswich Evening Star)*

With alacrity he parked his bike and hit the horse on the nose whereupon the horse reared and pushed its caravan into the car behind. A good Samaritan leading a goat across the road thought he could calm the animal. He tied his goat to the railway barrier and took hold of the frightened horse. Just then the crossing keeper raised the barriers to let traffic through—and hung the goat.

J. Graham *(Yorkshire Post)*

Pc Maureen Tomkinson said when Mrs Austin was asked by the policeman interviewing her if she had any birthmarks she pulled down her trousers and pants. Mrs Austin told the magistrates she had no intention of being indecent as she regarded policemen, like doctors, as asexual.

J. Stracey *(Hull Daily Mail)*

The Dahrein rioting was firmly crushed by the Saudi National Guard—an elite corpse which protects the ruling family.

J. Hudson *(Johannesburg Star)*

The Chester St. Cecelia Singers were further honoured last week by the BBC when television presenter, Gerald Harrison, invited them to take part in the programme "Let's have a good sin."

L. Considine *(Chester Chronicle)*

Elvis proposed to Ginger on his knees on January 26th last year, in the bathroom where seven months later he was found dead. "He loved to surprise me," she explained.

D. Vaullemin *(Woman)*

PEKING: China signed an agreement to buy 1,500,000 tonnes of what from Australia next year.

E. Pragnell *(Evening Standard)*

From the Oxford Almanack of 1782 showing from the Dean's Garden the Early English spire, so greatly admired by Ruskin, of the Cathedral of Christ Church. This is the best aspect of the building, which was stunted by the fall of Wolsey.

L. Babut *(Blackwell's Christmas Card)*

The report in yesterday's Age of a statement made before the Royal Commission on drugs was incorrect. The report, in indirect speech, quoted reformed heroin addict Kevin Beach as saying he got money by rolling drunks and stealing cars. A transcript shows that Mr Beach was asked whether he got money by rolling drunks and stealing FROM cars. Mr Beach answered in the affirmative.

G. Baker *(The Melbourne Age)*

Throwing caution to the winds, I ordered a tournedos (well done, with mixed salad and baked potatoes) and a half giraffe of wine.

F. Wynne *(Manchester Evening News)*

The funeral procession caused congestion at the Bullsmore Lane/A10 roundabout as a final tribute to Graham's sterling work for the Bullsmore Action Group.

S. Griffith *(Hornsey Independent)*

Prime Minister Joe Clark has no authority to propose bringing home the 1980 Summer Olympics to Montreal from Moscow, a Canadian Olympic Official said last night. Clark said yesterday he is seeking to have the Games moved because of the Soviet Union's invasion of Moscow.

B. Taggart *(Toronto Star)*

Corpses can't be carried as car pool passengers, a Marin judge ruled yesterday.

P. Rigby *(San Francisco Chronicle)*

Hard living, hard working millionaire television star David Janssen was about to change his lifestyle when he died suddenly last Wednesday.

J. Clarke *(Sydney Sun–Herald)*

HUGHES—Helen (nee Green) would like to thank Miss Johnson and the staff of Colwyn Bay Hospital and the many friends for flowers, gifts and many wishes and cards on my recent retirement. I would also like to say many grateful thanks to the surgical ward for the wonderful buffet.

J. Crofts *(North Wales Weekly)*

Ambulancemen grabbed arm of young man as he was about to jump six floors from top of Sunday Times building in Grays Inn Road and hauled him to safety. "We offered him a cup of tea but he said he wasn't falling for that."

F. Kordbarlag *(Evening News)*

For sale, parrot grey, talking, owner no longer shares parrots political opinions.

A. Fisher *(Times of Zambia)*

Mr Chapman said that when his team called in an Australian twin-engined helicopter to Ldave, the tribe "just clutched their piles—their most prized possessions—and looked on amazed as we lifted off."

R. Bailey *(Egyptian Gazette)*

A man was killed yesterday at Profitis Elias in Lamia as he was attempting to commit suicide, press sources revealed. LM, aged 65, was trying to hang himself from a tree but slipped and fell to the ground, injuring himself fatally.

R. Haynes *(Athens News)*

"A total of 101 coloured people became whites, one Chinese became a white, two whites received coloured classifications, six whites became Chinese, two whites became Indians, ten coloured people became Indians, 10 Malays became Indians, 11 Indians became coloured people, four Indians became Malays, three coloured people became Chinese while two Chinese were reclassified as coloured people."—A reply given by the Minister of the Interior to a question in Parliament last week.

J. Barnett *(Johannesburg Star)*

Mr David Hodsen, defending, said Johnson had been "fairly obnoxious" in the manner in which he had complained. Lee thought he was being insulated by Johnson who, he said, had challenged him to a fight.

R. Sweeny *(Oxford Times)*

Staging their first Derby Panto are director Michael Napier-Brown and Musical Director Andy Jubb, though they have appeared in these capacities here on other productions. A familiar figure in the pit from previous pantos will be Mike Sillitoe on drugs and percussion.

P. Jeffery *(West Notts Weekly Review)*

A cinema usherette turned to prostitution because the job proved too hard on her feet.

M. Kellehar *(Southend Evening Echo)*

Debbie is still good to watch because she is a very sexy and attractive lady but her voice wasn't consistent and at times you felt as though she wished she was anywhere she was.

A. Renton *(Essex Chronicle)*

Horse manure, hand picked, 40p per bag.

J. Bourne *(Western Gazette)*

Unemployed Patrick Foster spent almost £2,600 in a week on horses, beer and women. "I wasted the rest," he told detectives investigating a series of car frauds.

C. Church *(Middlesborough Evening Gazette)*

The Evening Mail, Birmingham, is launching a big development in its local news and advertising this week which will mean more local news and advertising.

Anon *(UK Press Gazette)*

Supporters of Pastor Jack Glass were moved from the front of Newlands South Church of Scotland as they protested against the appearance of Roman Catholic Archbishop Thomas Winning. The service heralding the beginning of the Week of Prayer for Christian Unity.

S. Turnbull *(Scottish Daily Record)*

Edinburgh and the Lothians suffered the heaviest December since records began.

R. Blackadder *(Scottish Sunday Express)*

Doctors at St Albans City Hospital will decide today whether there is any hope for a severely injured Harpenden.

J. Shelley *(St Albans Midweek Advertiser)*

(Dec 22—Jan 20): Nothing can go seriously wrong for you today, particularly auspicious one for goats who are participating in sports.

M. Oates *(Glasgow Daily Record)*

Carricks in Percy Street were fined £25 and ordered to pay £10 costs after they admitted selling soup with a fly in it. Mr Peter Watts, prosecuting, said the dead fly was discovered in a carton of soup bought by a woman. It had a leg missing.

A. Wright *(Newcastle Evening Chronicle)*

Coventry Aero Division's new Director and General Manager Peter Purden has been struck by the absolute friendliness of the Parkside workforce—and their evident sense of pride. "Not for one moment does anyone speak here without the firm conviction that Coventry is best," he said. Mr Burden, 48, is to move his home to Kenilworth.

D. Bacon *(Rolls-Royce News)*

Life in the island was hard with a severe shortage of food. The winter of 1944 was the worst with no gas, electricity or coal. Mrs N. Jackson was pianist and refreshments were served.

I. Winter *(Isle of Wight Weekly Post)*

More than 500 Ulster motorists will be in the dock soon after the weekend "no mercy" drive by the RUC to keep the Christmas roads safer. The promised clampdown on effing motorists resulted in 131 being charged with drunken driving.

J. Crawford *(Ulster Newsletter)*

How long are people going to talk about the color of eggs, what trivia, a waste of paper and manpower. I call it baby news. I remember my grandfather eating black painted eggs. Soon after he went away and I never found out why he did this.

R. Osbourne *(Melbourne Age)*

The plane hit short of the runway with a violent impact, bounced down again, veered left for 1,500 feet, and made a 180-degree turn before slamming to a stop. The main landing gear broke off, the No. 1 engine caught fire, part of the left wing sheared off, and the remainder was in flames. The hajji, being unfamiliar with planes, apparently took this for a normal landing.

R. Stallard *(Now!)*

But, brilliant though Picasso was, he was never heavyweight boxing champion of the Rhine Army; nor did he play tennis for Westmoreland.

J. Swiss *(British Gas)*

Shirley Morgan, aged 19, allegedly has told police in a statement that her husband, Brian, aged 20, forced her to write a suicide note after a violent row. He then ordered her to set the alarm clock for 7 am so he could get up early to kill her.

D. Potter (*Liverpool Daily Post*)

After warning an illegal camper to "move on", police then spent months trying to find him again so that he could be prosecuted.

D. Robertson (*The Scotsman*)

Police said Joe Basinger, a gas station attendant, was on duty late Friday when Larry Tate drove up and tried to rob him. Police said Tate told Basinger he had a gun in his pocket. Basinger refused to cooperate, police said, and Tate threatened to call police to force him. The attendant dared Tate to follow through on the threat and offered free use of the phone. Tate made the call and police arrived moments later and arrested him. "I think we would chalk it up to his being a little bit stupid," said police spokesman Vi Troxel.

M. Tapper (*Chicago Tribune*)

There were no objections by police at Uttoxeter magistrates court on Thursday when Inspector William Granville made an application for a licence extension for the town Police Club on the occasion of a stag night.

E. Harper (*The Uttoxeter Advertiser*)

John Lucas supped his umpteenth pint and boasted of being one of Britain's biggest dole collectors. "They've tried all sorts to get me to work," he said. "Three years ago I actually got a job with Sparks, the bakers. But I only stayed two days. They expected me to carry these really heavy cardboard boxes to an incinerator." He was most upset last week when he read that another man was hoping to get into the Guinness Book of Records because he's been out of work for 15 years. "I should be in rather than that bastard," he said. Everybody in Cameronian has a kind word for Mr Lucas. "He's got a heart of gold," said customer Arthur Stead. "He'll take a betting slip up to the shop for anyone."

E. Bell (*Northern Echo*)

Show business mogul Mr Robert Stigwood is now reported to be fully recovered after spending 36 hours in the intensive care unit of King Edward VII Memorial Hospital. He had been taken to the hospital by ambulance and admitted to intensive care where his illness had been "Quickly diagnosed as selfish poisoning".

T. K. Dyson (*Bermuda Royal Gazette*)

Major Eichler says tht 50% of the mothers who pass through Bethany decide to keep their babies. "Once it was opposite."

L. Sturch *(Auckland Star)*

SUNDAY JUNE 24 1979. Broadcast CHMM–Fm (97.5mg) 11:00 a.m. Dr. Vipond's and Dr. Conly's last service before retirement. Organ prelude—Now Thank We All Our God.

J. Fuller *(Westminster Church Bulletin, Winnipeg)*

WANTED—parrot cage for old age pensioner, around £5 please.

A. Lamb *(Leicester Trader)*

The wife of the councils chairman of Northants County Council, worth £3,000, was stolen from their home last year and has not been recovered.

F. Cooper *(Bedfordshire on Sunday)*

Dear Abby: I used to think you made up some of the letters in your column. I just couldn't believe that people could be so dumb. Now here I am, with a problem so unreal it sounds like a soap-opera plot. I am 23 and have been married for five years to Joe, a swell guy I've known for a year. This is my second marriage. I have three small children.
Frustrated in Russellville, Ark.
Dear Frustrated, No. You have a legitimate gripe. And may I suggest that those who can do their banking at another time please do so?

P. Brookes *(San Diego Union)*

When a check had been made on June 29th last year she had said that she was hoping to marry Barney O'Rourke in about three weeks. In fact the couple had been married on May 21st. Through the concealment of the marriage, said Mr Curnock, she had continued to draw benefit until early this year. Asked why she had not revealed the marriage, she said: "We had been married only two days when he punched me in the gob and left. I didn't think it worth reporting, would you?"

K. Rayment *(Lowestoft Journal)*

Star of the West End hit musical "Songbook", Dublin-born Gemma Craven has got the "needle"—to cure a back complaint which threatened her six-month run in the show. Causing her more distress than her back are the gossip mongers who claim she is Anton Rogers, who at 46 is 17 years her senior.

S. O'Grady *(Dublin Evening Herald)*

If Pearse was alive he'd be turning in his grave over the goings on in the Dail yesterday.   J. Sandeman *(The Irish Times)*

THE BEACON LUXURY CLUB. SPRING SPECTACULAR. Now on until 12th May. Tues. "Special Night Out"—Normal activities. Thurs. "Big Night Out"—Normal Activities.
T. Moss *(Shepherds Bush Gazette)*

"In addition to these attributes, common to all the best latex tubes, the Imp'Air Latex tube has another advantage—it holds air indefinitely (but not quite as long as butyl tube)."
A. Larrad *(Cycling)*

Gill Sargeant. Married with two children. Came to Swindon from Manchester. Seeking election because she is concerned about the lack of local people in local government.
M. Harle *(Swindon Evening Advertiser)*

This is Santa's first visit to Edlington and weather permitting, he will tour the streets of Edlington to arrive at his ghetto at (S & N's) at 2 p.m. on Saturday 26th.
D. Stubbs *(Doncaster Advertiser)*

A 28-year-old American is trying to get the British interested in keeping pigs as pets. He says they are more intelligent than dogs and cleaner than cats. Mr Steve Zlotowitz has two 15-week-old pigs on sale for £10 each—but he cannot find the right buyer. He said: "I don't like the way people are licking their lips when they look at them."
N. Flock *(Yorkshire Post)*

Bird experts were flying high when they heard that a rare stone curlew had been spotted. They hoped to reclaim the bird's body for their records after it was shot in mistake for a duck, but all they got was its wings and legs—retrieved from a Suffolk family's dustbin. The family told the experts from the British Trust for Ornithology: "It tasted very good."
F. Martell *(Sheffield Morning Telegraph)*

He wants to open a bistro in former shop premises at the bottom of Castle Hill, Banwell. With cautious provincialism, Woodspring planners have deferred his application because members admitted they were not quite certain what a bistro is.
H. Gray *(Central Somerset Gazette)*

CHURCH FILLED FOR BAPTISM
R. Wood *(The Bury Free Press)*

The first topless barmaid in Wales who was arrested just 20 minutes after starting the job was appealing in a London court today. She faces three charges of criminal deception.

K. Geldard (*Yorkshire Evening Post*)

A man looking for work indecently exposed himself to a woman at the Ipswich Department of Health and Social Security because he thought it might help him to get a job.

G. Russell (*Ipswich Evening Star*)

When police came across unemployed labourer Thomas O'Grady in a Cliftonville bank late one October night they asked him what he was doing and he replied: "I've come about my overdraft."

D. Rigby (*East Kent Times*)

After a string of television appearances—she spent a year in Crossroads, but now feels much better—she has become one of television's most sought-after leading ladies.

C. Smallhorn (*Liverpool Echo*)

Ambrose would like to be a policeman, but wasn't too taken with the "barracks" where cadets in training stay. "He's loved the police for years," said his mother Mrs Phil Hogan. "We think it's rather strange."

J. Coles (*St Alban's Review*)

Israeli jets last night launched a three hour attack on an old people's home in Torquay.

B. Lacey (*Hereford Evening News*)

Concentrated butter for cooking will soon be in Britain's shops, at about 32½p a half pound. The butter—from which all butter has been removed—is widely used in other Common Market countries.

B. Ford (*Western Daily Press*)

Edward Heath took some guests by surprise when he opened Brighton Marina's yacht club last week. They were struck by a resemblance remarkable to a real human being.

U. Strong (*Brighton and Hove Gazette*)

The only other programme affected was Cilla Black's show, which was replaced by a musical show.

T. Barnsley (*Yorkshire Post*)

Tuesday: DISCO NIGHT for sophisticated people only. Free hot-pot supper.

J. Brian (*Stockport Express*)

Mr Stone slammed some doctors for coming up with all sorts of conditions for workers affected by alcoholism. "I'm convinced some can't even spell the word alcoholims."

R. Davis *(The Adelaide News)*

Prime Minister Joe Clark has no authority to propose bringing home the 1980 Summer Olympics to Montreal from Moscow, a Canadian Olympic Official said last night. Clark said yesterday he is seeking to have the Games moved because of the Soviet Union's invasion of Moscow.

B. Taggart *(Toronto Star)*

Plans to break the world flame throwing record at James Brothers Circus in Waltham Cross hit a snag on Wednesday morning when 26-year-old Karl Alva sucked instead of blew in training.

B. Eggs *(Lea Valley Mercury)*

Hurt is an actor of resourceful sensitivity. "I have been told I seem to play only eccentrics but I don't think the parts I have played are any more eccentric than Malvolio in Twelfth Night or the Foot in Lear."

D. Yates *(Liverpool Daily Post)*

There are advertisements between overs and from time to time irritating little captains moving right to left across the screen exhorting you to buy a certain brand of beer.

T. Leckie-Brunton *(Sydney Herald)*

UN Security Council members are ready to give Iran up to five days to respond to Tuesday's resolution calling for the freezing of US hostages.

P. Wray *(Philippines Bulletin Today)*

Hurt is an actor of resourceful sensitivity. "I have been told I seem to play only eccentrics but I don't think the parts I have played are any more eccentric than Malvolio in Twelfth Night or the Foot in Lear."

D. Yates *(Liverpool Daily Post)*

CAPE TOWN—Surgeons here have grafted a man's feet to the stumps of his things after amputating his lower legs.

E. Zahedi *(Kayhan International)*

It's true they didn't live up to the high standards set by director and choreographer Maive Hewson, once a danger in the original London production in the 50s.

D. Rowe *(Wickford Evening Echo)*

McEwan, who asked for 98 cases to be tried separately in August, said he was now unemployed: "I'm not worth employing. I spend so much time in court."

D. Barber *(Slough Observer)*

BLADON HOUSE SCHOOL. Residential, maladjusted HOUSEMASTER required as soon as possible.

C. Bamford *(Burton Daily Mail)*

Six Shanghai street gangsters have been sentenced to up to eight years in jail for attacking passers-by when another gang failed to keep a battle appointment.

P. Ward *(Glasgow Herald)*

Smith, a politics student at Grey College, told the court: "I didn't think they would believe my name was Smith because I had no identification on me so I told them it was Jones."

E. Scott *(Hartlepool Mail)*

But, brilliant though Picasso was, he was never heavyweight boxing champion of the Rhine Army; nor did he play tennis for Westmoreland.

J. Swiss *(British Gas)*

Mr McKinlay added that the dances the club held were run purely for club funds and not for social pleasure.

S. Welsh *(Milngavie and Bearsden Herald)*

Omitted from the funeral of Mr David Gibbon which appeared in our last edition were the Revs. W. Harry and J. C. Jones, both of whom were unable to attend.   M. Blayney *(Western Telegraph)*

New Group Product Manager at KP Foods is John Koster, previously with Kentucky Fried Children.

M. Keith *(Supermarketing)*

SHORTER POLICE SUGGESTED FOR UNDERSIZE FORCE.

W. Rowland *(Yorkshire Post)*

A man climbed into a haystack where he made himself an alcove and lit a fire to keep warm, York Crown Court heard today.

G. Steadman *(Yorkshire Evening Press)*

Mr Pudney's affection for the village was mirrored in the number of times he had been found drunk in Madingly Road.

A. Raynger *(Cambridge Evening News)*

Andrew Richard Mann, 17, of Campbell Drive, Carlton, is charged with unlawfully killing Gary Sean Donnelly at Mapperley on January 15, and with murdering him on January 16.

J. Edwards (*Nottingham Evening Post*)

The Red Lion, Desford. Tel. Desford 2279. We are pleased to announce that due to the popularity of our mid-week specials, we are now extending this to cover Tuesdays, Wednesdays and Thursdays.

C. A. Merrill (*Leicester Mercury*)

A set of traffic lights has been stolen from a main road junction in Reading. A police spokesman said: "Some thieves will stop at nothing."

C. Collins (*Southend Evening Echo*)

The pollen count in the Leeds area yesterday was expected to stay in that vicinity today.

M. Robinson (*Yorkshire Post*)

An elderly woman up from the country spent three days trying to get out of a hypermarket in Utrecht, Holland, police said today. The 70-year-old woman had gone shopping with her sister at the Hoog Catherijne complex of 200 stores. She lost her sister in the pre-Easter crowd and then wandered around the complex for three days trying to find the exit. The woman told police she was afraid to ask other shoppers how to get out.

H. Jacobs (*Birmingham Evening Mail*)

Apsley's first ever Community Day was hit by hazards when the hot-air balloon wouldn't go up, the ponies for the children's rides never arrived and the police display team were called away to the pop festival at Knebworth. On top of that the Judo Club didn't turn up and no one entered the beauty contest. Said organiser Mrs Pat Jones: "It was a great success. We're going to do it again next year."

J. Elworthy (*Hemel Hempstead Star*)

A Leyton woman advised at a psychiatric unit to work her anger and frustration out on paper was jailed at the Old Bailey on Thursday for sending a death message to a policewoman.

M. Crofts (*Waltham Forest Guardian*)

The Association is now in its 90th anniversary year. It is, they claim, England's oldest. It may also have been the first.

J. Smith (*Lancashire Life*)

The Pollen count at 10 a.m. today was one, which is very low.

E. Mungall (*Yorkshire Evening Press*)

The alternative route for persons passing from Tan y Grisiau Road to the new A496 is to proceed in a southerly direction along Tan y Grisiau Road for a distance of 233 yards, turn left and proceed in an easterly direction for a distance of 133 yards along footpath 77; turn left and proceed in a northerly direction along the A496 for a distance of 316 yards; turn left again to proceed along the said Footpath 84 for a distance of 166 yards; and vice versa for people proceeding in the opposite direction.

G. Auckland *(Caernavon and Denbigh Herald)*

From 1951 to 1968, Dr Carlson was medical officer for Drayton Hall maternity home and held a similar post with Norwich Rugby Football Club between 1953 and this year.

D. Bottomley *(Eastern Evening News)*

"Art brings about thoughts of fornication and adultery," said Barry Masimer, 28 years old, a member of the religious group. "I used to live in a fantasy world because of books, movies and art." The sect also opposes Social Security, Medicare, unemployment, insurance, doctors, hospitals, medicines, alcohol, tobacco, jewelry, drugs, dancing, neckties, cologne, haircuts, dating, Halloween, Easter and Christmas.

J. Garland *(New York Times)*

The commissioner was commenting on the allegations made by a prisoner at the Lusaka Central Prison, who charged that the recent escape at the prison was due to inefficiency and maladministration on the part of prison authorities, and by eight detainees who also claimed that they were being treated like convicts. At present, he said, there were only about 2,000 guarding 10,000 prisoners throughout the country and yet to effectively control the crime rate the department needs to have one officer for every five inmates. He asked: "How can somebody say that he has been beaten up by a warder, but when opening his mouth you find that all his teeth are there?"

A. Featherstone *(Zambia Daily Mail)*

A meal for two there these days will come to about £7 a head without food.

R. Tree *(Where to Go In London)*

The crowd of 40,00 responded enthusiastically to the orchestra, led by Harry Ellis, the assistant to the late Arthur Fiedler, who was unable to make the concert due to poor health.

T. Smith *(Connecticutt Daily Campus)*

Van driver required, aged 25 or over, clean licence, ability to handle money and hamper work.

S. Bartlett *(Hastings and St Leonards Observer)*

Haggis is normally eaten with mashed neeps (turnips). There were approximately 36 people present at the club's supper, of whom about half were Sots.

J. Blomely *(Wokingham Times)*

A self-employed roofing contractor, who started his firm with no experience and then discovered he suffered from virtigo, was adjudged bankrupt at Swansea's County Court yesterday.

T. Field *(South Wales Evening Post)*

Evans, a Welsh international, was fined for alleged misbehaviour on stage in the Embassy World Championships and has appealed. The appeal is due to be heard on Saturday and local farts fanatics will be hoping for a happy outcome.

D. Williamson *(Oldham Evening Chronicle)*

FOR SALE. Oak coffin, unwanted Christmas present £25.

G. Martin *(Bordon Herald)*

Some of our friends who made regular subscriptions have died during the year, but we would like to think that there are others who would consider doing the same.

A. Tull *(Thorner Parish Magazine)*

His wife, Mary Lou Robinson, charged with aiding and abetting him, was given a conditional discharge for one year. "We're sorry it won't happen again," she told magistrates.

W. Keen *(Leamington Spa Courier)*

A man charged with tearing down a UANC election poster claimed at Dett Magistrates Court yesterday that when he saw the poster he was so overcome with love for Bishop Muzorewa he hugged the tree to which it was tied and inadvertently pulled it down.

C. Hingley *(Bulawayo Chronicle)*

The woman, wearing a green skirt, blue jumper and with white hair wasn't instantly recognisable from her husband's description of a dark-haired woman clad in a red skirt and white jumper. "The description the husband gave of her is probably the one when he married her," a police spokesman said.

L. Bolton *(Melbourne Sun)*

A liquor store was looted and police opened fire after they were stoned.

N. Harding *(Cape Times)*

It's no wonder young Hayes songstress Elizabeth Bryant has a good voice—her grandfather was Bing Crosby's second cousin.

J. Maling *(Hayes Gazette)*

A Tory councillor hid in a chimney piece for 20 minutes at the City Chambers in Glasgow yesterday to help his party fight off a bid by Labour to remove them from power.

E. Jack *(Glasgow Herald)*

Contraceptive Services Section (ref. C.1.) The successful applicant, who will enjoy working with figures, will be responsible for the preparation of the statement for payment of a specified group of general practitioners. In both cases, appropriate on the job training will be given.

C. Alleeson *(Hillingdon Mirror)*

There will be a procession next Sunday afternoon in the grounds of the Monastery; but if it rains in the afternoon the procession will take place in the morning.

A. Burkinshaw *(Irish Parish Bulletin)*

ENTERTAINMENTS: Clown Joey. Please see obituary column.

N. Milner *(Oxford Times)*

The 400-year-old teacher at the Ulster Polytechnic paints landscapes which are abstract in a way, and for some reason turn out looking very well.

P. Sheehan *(Dublin Evening Herald)*

Four eunuchs at a Pratpgarh polling centre refused to cast their votes on finding that they had been listed as males. They said in the last two elections, they had voted on being assured that they would be listed as "females" next time. They clapped and waved their hands in their usual style as they left the booth.

W. Kani *(Hindustan Times)*

Duck wins title of Bahrain's fastest man.

S. Boothroyd *(Gulf Mirror)*

Odd sized feet. Man with odd sized feet, right foot $6\frac{1}{2}/7$, left foot $8\frac{1}{2}/9$ wishes to contact someone with similar problem but preferably with shoe sizes reversed with view to joint buying.

J. Akhurst *(South Wales Echo)*

The Government will soon introduce a law which will stipulate the minimum alcoholic content in the blood of a person required to drive a motor vehicle.

R. Major *(Zambia Daily Mail)*

The lure of the bright lights and valuable recording contracts do not interest Mid-Bedfordshire's newest country and western group Country Ribbon. The group usually play at the Mid-Bedfordshire Conservative Club and although they don't really want to hit the big time they do like a bit of variety and recently had a booking at the Houghton Conquest Village Hall.

S. Yorke *(Luton Evening Post)*

A Bucks County Council project costing £10,000 to give work experience for unemployed youngsters looks like being abandoned due to a shortage of unemployed youngsters. Only four were interested, but one joined the merchant navy, one fell off his motor cycle and the other two failed to turn up.

M. Eyles *(Bucks Free Press)*

Golders Green A.B.C. 2 "The Bitch" (X)
Hammersmith A.B.C. 2 "The Botch" (X)

M. Girling *(Time Out)*

A lady medical graduate from India with 3 years Gynaecology and Obstetrics seeks suitable opening.

H. McGarry *(Khaleej Times)*

For the first time in Danish police history a parrot has been questioned as a witness.

G. Ridgewell *(Watford Evening Echo)*

Lucas produce a completely pointless distributor to fit most cars.

M. Atkins *(Hot Car)*

Syston police would like to hear from anyone who say anything suspicious.

C. Merrill *(Leicester Mercury)*

The mutilated "dog" found hanging from a tree in Bog Wood, near Penicuik, at the weekend was actually a fox, Lothian and Borders police reported yesterday. They are no longer anxious to hear from anyone who has lost a light-coloured whippet.

N. Braidwood *(The Scotsman)*

Rufus Owen Watts Sr. has been re-elected to the Halifax County Democratic Committee, but he won't serve his term. Watts has been dead for more than a year. County party Chairman Howard P. Anderson said Watts was re-elected because the committee has a policy of "not dumping" members who have served faithfully.

D. Goldberg *(Los Angeles Times)*

Obviously the Edmonton Symphony Orchestra (ESO) is going to have a new music director. Most likely it will have more than one if the average tenure is any criteria. My forecast is for a larger orchestra, because I am convinced the symphony has got to get more people to its concerts.

P. Metzies *(Edmonton Journal)*

Zambia wastes about 50 per cent of her food each year after harvest and before consumption. President Kaunda last year canned Zambians for the wastage of food.

A. Taylor *(Times of Zambia)*

AIR BVI REQUIRES STEWARDESSES for immediate employment. Minimum age 17 years. Must be in good health and be able to swim.

S. Dick-Read *(British Virgin Islands Sun)*

A Swiss housewife broke two records when she flew to the Isle of Skye for a holiday. She was the first woman to land solo on the island and the first pilot to have an accident at the 2600 yard Ashaig airstrip.

M. Stead *(The Scotsman)*

Sainsbury's, the London-based food giants, have taken their first steps towards building a giant supersore in the centre of Crosby.

A Stewart *(Crosby Herald)*

"David Bowie is one of a dying breed who'll live on forever."

P. Gray *(New Musical Express)*

Greek millionairess Christina Onassis, apparently settled down to matrimony with her Russian husband, Sergei, went shipping for groceries last week.

R. Hough *(Akhbar Oman)*

An interesting talk on the *Jewish Family Life* was given to the N.A.W.C. Molehurst, last week. The speaker, Mr Donald Trennent said : "Belief in God, is the basic rule for Jewish people, which began with Abraham. Foods which were forbidden in the Jewish faith were pig, rabbi and camel."

F. Davies *(Esher Borough News)*

Lauren Bacall can count her television dramatic appearances on her fingers, and Friday's guest shot on "The Rockford Files" will be No. 12.

D. Collins *(Washington Post)*

Plans to convert a Great Baddow Church to central heating have been scrapped on orders from above.

C. Read *(Woodham and Wickford Chronicle)*

The Roman Catholic Archdiocese of New York has joined a group of Orthodox rabbits in condemning the "Life of Brian."

M. Davison *(Caracas Daily Journal)*